Best-Ever
Activities for Grades 2-3

Listening & Speaking

Dozens of Activities With Engaging Reproducibles That Kids Will Love...From Creative Teachers Across the Country

BY BOB KRECH

SCHOLASTIC
PROFESSIONAL BOOKS

New York • Toronto • London • Auckland • Sydney • Mexico City
New Delhi • Hong Kong • Buenos Aires

For Margaret Strucker and Lois Walker, two great teachers

Many thanks to all the creative contributors: Deborah Bauer, Karen Bjork, Jackie Clarke, Kathryn Lay, Lyn MacBruce, Evan Milman, Randi Mrvos, Deborah Versfeld, Judy Wetzel, and Wendy Wise-Borg. Thanks again to my two artists-in-residence, Andrew and Faith Krech.

"Sounds" by M. Lucille Ford from POETRY PLACE ANTHOLOGY (Scholastic, 1990).

Every effort has been made by the publisher to locate the author of this poem and to secure the necessary permissions. If there are any questions regarding the use of this poem, the publisher will take appropriate corrective measures to acknowledge ownership in future editions.

Scholastic Inc. grants teachers permission to photocopy the designated reproducible pages from this book for classroom use. No other part of this publication may be reproduced in whole or in part, or stored in a retrieval system, or transmitted in any form or by any means, electronic, mechanical, photocopying, recording, or otherwise, without written permission of the publisher. For information regarding permission, write to Scholastic Inc., 557 Broadway, New York, NY 10012.

Produced by **Joan Novelli**
Cover and interior design by **Holly Grundon**
Cover and interior art by **Paige Billin-Frye**

ISBN 0-439-30946-8

CONTENTS

CONTENTS

About This Book

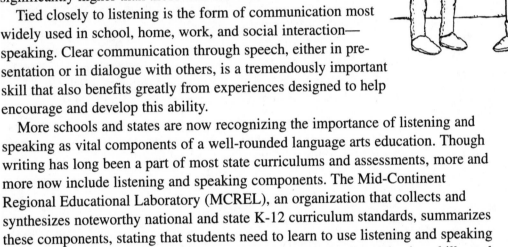

What do children spend more than half of their school day doing? Reading? Math? Talking? Actually, the answer is listening! According to one study, 57.5 percent of an elementary child's school day is spent listening. Yet the ability to listen is often taken for granted, even though research shows that students who have had structured learning experiences to promote listening have performance scores significantly higher than those who have not.

Tied closely to listening is the form of communication most widely used in school, home, work, and social interaction— speaking. Clear communication through speech, either in presentation or in dialogue with others, is a tremendously important skill that also benefits greatly from experiences designed to help encourage and develop this ability.

More schools and states are now recognizing the importance of listening and speaking as vital components of a well-rounded language arts education. Though writing has long been a part of most state curriculums and assessments, more and more now include listening and speaking components. The Mid-Continent Regional Educational Laboratory (MCREL), an organization that collects and synthesizes noteworthy national and state K-12 curriculum standards, summarizes these components, stating that students need to learn to use listening and speaking strategies for different purposes, use a variety of verbal communication skills, and use strategies to enhance listening comprehension.

The activities in this book provide opportunities to teach and assess these skills in fun and creative ways. Many integrate more than one skill from across the disciplines. For example, In the News strengthens listening skills, while also giving students a chance to practice writing skills and keep up on current events. (See page 27.) Weather Report builds speaking skills and strengthens science skills and concepts at the same time. (See page 13.) Other highlights of the book include:

- activities from teachers across the country
- support for the many ways your students learn, including activities that link listening and speaking with writing, art, music, and movement
- strategies for second-language learners
- computer connections

- test-taking and assessment tips
- literature connections
- graphic organizers
- take-home activity sheets
- ready-to-use reproducible activity sheets
- and more activities to enhance listening and speaking goals in your language arts program and beyond!

Sentence Scramblers

Careful listening is a must when you scramble the words in a spoken sentence and students have to figure out what you said.

⊚ Say a sentence aloud, but mix up the word order. For example, you might say, "I brown like shoes your" instead of "I like your brown shoes."

⊚ Ask students to listen to the scrambled sentence and then write the words in the correct order.

⊚ Invite a volunteer to read the sentence aloud and share a listening strategy—for example, good posture, eyes on speaker, and mentally repeating what you heard. Repeat the activity with a few other scrambled sentences, each time sharing a listening strategy.

⊚ Have students work with partners to make up scrambled sentences of their own. Let them share them with the class for more listening and unscrambling. "Class your fun will have!"

Sounds Like a Poem!

What does a poem sound like? Have your students try this listening activity to find out!

Select a place in your school—for example, the classroom, cafeteria, playground, or library. With clipboards in hand, take your students to this location and have them listen very carefully for a few minutes. Ask them to record any sounds they hear. Let students share the sounds on their lists. Record them on chart paper, leaving off any duplicate sounds. Use the sounds to write a class list poem, listing the sounds line by line and ending with "Sounds like [fill in the place]!" It's great to try this with two very different places that provide a vivid contrast in the sorts of sounds one might hear. Imagine trying this in the library and then in the cafeteria at lunchtime!

Number Listening

Students find out that pennies dropped in a can make a loud sound—but they still have to listen carefully to count them.

- Display an empty coffee can and some pennies. Provide students with pencils and paper.

- Stand behind students (students facing away from you) and direct them not to turn around and to listen carefully. Explain that you are going to be dropping pennies in the can and you want everyone to listen very carefully to determine how many you drop all together. Have students keep tallies to show how many pennies they hear as you drop them.

- Let students physically count the coins to check their answers. Repeat the activity, changing the rate and rhythm of the coin drop. You might also let children trade seats with one another to listen from another spot in the room.

For greater mathematical challenges, switch to dimes, quarters, or other coins and ask for totals.

That's the Answer. What's the Question?

It's fun to play around with words and sentences. It helps give children a feeling of mastery and control of language. This activity boosts listening and speaking skills, too.

Read aloud a statement—for example, "He was already asleep." Have students discuss the sentence in small groups and create questions that would elicit this target statement as an answer. A suitable question for "He was already asleep" might be "Why didn't he come out to play?" Let groups take turns sharing their questions orally and reading the answer immediately after. Ask the rest of the class to listen and give feedback about how well the questions and answers match up.

Because He Loved Her

Students tune in to hear what the hero in this progressive song/poem/chant does next. You can repeat the activity any number of times, with different results each time.

Gather children in a circle. Explain that you are going to say the first part of a statement and that they will chime in on the second part: "because he loved her." Say something like "He ate thirty apples…" or "He wrestled armadillos all night long…." Then have children add the ending ("…because he loved her"). Let the child to your right take a turn, offering a line about the hero and having classmates finish the sentence with "…because he loved her." Students can feel free to come up with serious or silly lines—their classmates can say the ending with feeling either way.

Literature LINK

Book of Riddles

by Bennett Cerf (Random House, 1960)

Share some age-appropriate riddles from this (or another) collection. Discuss with the class what makes a good riddle, then let students try sharing some of their own. Ask students to think of an object, person, or place. Have them write down five clues about their selection. Clues that are progressively more specific work well. Let students take turns reading aloud their riddles and letting classmates guess the answer after each clue. If no one guesses by the last clue, the author reveals the answer.

Blind Directions

This twist on a classic listening activity is always a great way to fill a few spare moments or to provide a skill-building break between longer activities.

Pair up students and have them sit back to back in their chairs. Give each child a sheet of paper and pencil. Have one child in each set of partners draw a simple design on the paper, using only six straight lines. This child then describes the design to his or her partner so that the child can replicate it. Students must remain back to back during the entire process. Students then compare diagrams to see how close the original and replica are. Which directions worked well? Which didn't? What else would have been helpful to know? Have students switch places and try the activity again.

As students become more proficient at explaining clearly and listening carefully, they can try increasingly complex figures.

Puppet Talk

Some students find it very difficult to speak in front of others, even their own classmates. Puppets are one way to help ease students into public speaking.

Bring in or make a puppet to introduce to students. (It's always fun to have a class puppet in hand—one that occasionally pipes in at the morning meeting, gives directions, shares a story, and so on.) Allow time for students to talk to the puppet. (They almost always readily will.) After the class gets used to your puppet, invite them to bring in puppets or stuffed animals of their own to meet and converse with the class puppet. This playacting provides lots of fun opportunities for speaking and listening in a relaxed atmosphere. Children can then move on to give speeches with their puppets, paving the way for an increased comfort level with speaking independently (without puppet props) in front of others.

Judy Wetzel
Woodburn School
Falls Church, Virginia

Telephone

A game of Telephone is a great opportunity for teaching the importance of active listening.

After sharing the story *The Surprise Party* (see below), provide a similar experience for students by playing the game Telephone. Gather children in a seated circle, and whisper a message to a student to your left. Have that child whisper the message to the next child, who will repeat it to the next student, and so on, around the circle. Take this opportunity to teach children the strategy of active listening. Through active listening, each student repeats what the first person said to make sure the message was understood.

Jackie Clarke
Cicero Elementary
Cicero, New York

Literature LINK

The Surprise Party

by Pat Hutchins (Macmillan, 1969)

This book begins, "'I'm having a surprise party tomorrow,' whispered Rabbit. 'It's a surprise.'" Unfortunately, the animal he whispered it to thought he said, "Rabbit is hoeing the parsley tomorrow." As the message is passed on, it gets more and more mixed up. A natural followup to the story, of course, is a game of Telephone. (See above.)

The Listening Box

A closed box with something rattling around inside is always intriguing. Students will listen ever so carefully as they try to figure out what's inside. This activity works well with a unit about the senses or when used regularly with science lessons to investigate new materials.

- Separately wrap the lid and bottom of a small box. Add a ribbon to the lid for effect.
- Show students a list of six to ten small objects—a marble, key, coin, bead, eraser, and so on. Have students close their eyes while you place one of those objects inside the box.
- Shake, move, and rattle the box while students listen carefully to identify the object. Give them as many chances to guess as you like, then repeat the activity with a new object.

Literature LINK

Drummer Hoff

by Barbara Emberley (Simon & Schuster, 1967)

This picture book features Caldecott-winning illustrations by Ed Emberley and offers lots of noise, action, and rhyme. Listening for rhyme helps students with reading. It provides a pattern and structure that enhance comprehension. In this story, various members of the army help get the cannon ready for firing. Their names rhyme with the action in each sequence and are fun to read aloud. After reading the story, invite students to help you create a class book that uses their own names in rhyme. You can use first and/or last names, whatever works well with the rhyming and subjects. For example, you might end up with something like this: "Young John Jones ate all the cones" or "Tina Salmastrelli rubbed her belly." Have each student write and illustrate a sentence for the story. Combine these in a book and enjoy reading it aloud together.

For a really fun homework assignment, have students make their own Listening Box to share with the class. Send home guidelines so that families are aware of the sorts of things students might put inside the box.

Public Speaking Self-Check

It's a good idea to get children to self-assess in any area. Here's a checklist-type rubric you can develop with students to evaluate their own public speaking.

- Ask students to share what they know about public speaking—for example, when they share at morning meeting, what do they need to remember? Students might suggest the following: speaking loudly enough to be heard by all, speaking clearly, speaking slowly, looking at people when they speak, waiting their turn to speak, using expression, and using gestures.

- Record students' ideas on chart paper or the chalkboard, then use them to create a self-assessment rubric.

- Encourage students to complete the rubric after giving class presentations. Have them date and keep the evaluations. Compare earlier checklists with later ones to let students see how their speaking skills have grown.

Deborah Versfeld
Village School
Princeton Junction, New Jersey

TiP

This type of rubric is very useful for helping students prepare for and evaluate presentations in any subject area.

Literature
LINK

Arthur Meets the President

by Marc Brown (Little, Brown, 1991)

Arthur enters a national essay contest and wins! Now he must recite his essay before the President of the United States. At the last moment, the President's helicopter creates a wind that blows the notecards out of Arthur's hands. Can his precocious little sister, D.W., save the day for Arthur? Students engaged in organizing their own talks will relate to Arthur's situation as he brainstorms, writes, and prepares his speech.

A Special Place

Here's an assignment that gets everyone listening (and writing and thinking, too).

Tell students that for homework they will need to write about a special place. Ask them to write at least five sentences that describe this place, but not to name it. Encourage them to use their senses as they describe the place, considering how it smells, feels, looks, and sounds. There may even be things to taste there. Have students write their descriptive sentences on an index card or sheet of paper. When they bring their writing to class, let students take turns sharing their pieces with the class. Can the audience guess the place the writer has described?

Kathryn Lay
Homeschool Teacher
Arlington, Texas

Weather Report

Weather is important to kids. Their main concern is whether they'll be able to play outside; even so, that's a big consideration for a second- or third-grader. Tap into this interest by letting students take turns sharing the weather report.

☉ Assign each student a day to be the class weather reporter. Write the schedule on the class calendar so that students know when their turn is coming.

☉ To prepare for their weather report, students will need to listen to a local weather report for the day and take some notes.

☉ Give students time to practice their presentations before sharing them with the class (or even with the school over the public address system). Encourage students to add their own advice about how to dress for the following day, such as "Tomorrow will be cold and windy, so be sure to wear a warm jacket!"

Karen Bjork
Portage Public Schools
Portage, Michigan

Something Missing?

In this activity, students need to listen carefully to find out what is missing.

- Have students work in pairs to choose a well-known song, poem, jingle, or rhyme. Explain that they need to write down all the words (or the words to the first few lines of a longer song) and then erase one word. For example, they might choose "The Star Spangled Banner" and write "Oh, say can you see, __ the dawn's early light" (having erased the word *by*).

- Have students present the piece to the class, by singing, reciting, or reading it. Remind them to leave out one word. The task of the audience is to listen very carefully and try to identify either from memory or context what the missing word is.

Crazy Topic Picks

For some fun and quick thinking anytime, try a Crazy Topic Picks session. Students will enjoy creating these silly presentations, and their classmates will have even more fun listening.

- Fill a fish bowl or other container with small folded pieces of paper. On each paper, write a fun topic such as "My Life on Mars" or "Why Chocolate Should Be Eaten at Every Meal."

- At the beginning of a Topic Pick session, let a few students each choose a topic from the bowl. They should then work for the rest of the period preparing a two- or three-minute speech on the topic, writing simple notes on index cards to organize their ideas.

- Give students time to present their silly speeches. Record them on cassette or videotape for a great collection that students may enjoy sharing on open-school night.

Lyn MacBruce
Randolph Elementary School
Randolph, Vermont

Buddy Book and Tape

It's highly motivating and very focusing to write for a specific audience, particularly an appreciative audience. Here's a long-term project that combines writing, speaking, and listening skills, while giving second- or third-graders a chance to share with younger children.

- Explain to students that they will be writing a book of their choice and that the book will be for a younger audience, either kindergarten or first grade. Share some examples of age-appropriate picture books on which children can model their books.

- Over a period of time, have students write and illustrate their books. Help them make a durable cover and bind the pages with book-binding tape or staples.

- With the help of a parent aide or in a one-on-one meeting, have students tape-record their stories as they read the book aloud.

- As a culminating activity, set up a special day for your class to meet the younger class. Have your students buddy up with the younger children and read their books aloud.

Karen Bjork
Portage Public Schools
Portage, Michigan

Target Note-Taking

When students watch an informational video or presentation, make sure they get the most out of it and build listening skills with "target note-taking."

Before a lesson or presentation, share your objectives with students. For example, let's say you're studying Antarctica and as part of the lesson, students will be watching a video. Tell students which ideas you want them specifically to focus on, such as: Who were the early explorers of Antarctica? What kinds of animals live in Antarctica? Does Antarctica have a government? Have students jot down these questions on a sheet of paper, to serve as a viewing and listening guide. As they listen, encourage students to take notes that relate to any of the questions. This will help them focus on the important content and retain information you want them to learn.

TIP

At the end of the session, students can present their tapes and books to the kindergarten or first-grade teacher to keep as part of the class library. The younger children will enjoy borrowing and listening to their older buddies' tapes and books.

Listening for Directions

Most standardized tests include a set of directions read aloud by the teacher. These directions are sometimes not written anywhere, and students most likely will hear them only once. Students must listen carefully in order to know what it is they are to do in the testing situation. This is a format unfamiliar to most students and it can catch many off guard. Share this test-taking tip to help prepare students.

To familiarize students with testing procedures in which directions are read aloud, run an occasional practice test following this format:

Tell students that you will be reading the directions only once and that they will not be written anywhere.

Remind them that they will only hear them the one time. Urge them to visualize what they are to do as the directions are read.

Providing students with a few short experiences like this will help familiarize them with this method so they will be ready when they encounter it again in more formal testing situations.

Interactive Morning Message:
Good Morning, Judge

Your students listen to each other all the time, every day, all day long, so they probably know what everybody sounds like. Or do they? Take turns once a week trying this listening skill-building activity.

Have students close their eyes and put their heads down on their desks. Now tap three students on the shoulders and have them move quietly to the front of the room. With the other students remaining heads down, eyes closed, point to one of the three students and have him or her say, "Good Morning, Judge." The student can disguise his or her voice if desired. After hearing the student, the rest of the students open their eyes and try to guess which one of the three was the speaker. Make sure to give everyone a turn to be the speaker, then repeat the activity with new students.

When handing out a homework assignment, make an overhead copy of the sheet. Give this special overhead copy to one student, along with an erasable overhead marker pen. This student will complete the homework assignment on the overhead sheet, then use it to lead the "homework checking" the next day.

Million Dollar Word

The idea of a million of anything is always appealing to students, and with this activity they'll be sure to listen for a word that's worth a million dollars.

Subscribe to the word-of-the-day at **www.word central.com**. Each entry includes the word's part of speech, definition, usage, and synonyms.

At the beginning of the day, select a target word and introduce it to the class. Write the word on the board, then give a definition and discuss the word. Then tell the class that the word is the Million Dollar Word for the day. Ask students to listen carefully throughout the day for the Million Dollar Word. Whenever they hear it, have them give a special signal, such as putting their hand on top of their head or holding up a pretend dollar bill. Try to use the word at least twice during the day. See how many students remember, listen, and key in when the word is spoken.

SOLAR Graphic Organizer

There are several acronyms to help students remember good listening skills. SOLAR is an easy one.

Ask students what they think the letters SOLAR might stand for. Let them guess for a while, then share that they stand for: sit (or stand) up straight (S), open posture (O), lean forward (L), ask questions (A), and repeat what you heard (R). On chart paper, write the acronym and the listening tips for which it stands. Invite a volunteer to help you model each listening skill for the class. Stand with this child in front of the class and have a brief conversation. Be sure to clearly demonstrate what each letter stands for. Have students identify the skills each gesture represents. Now model another conversation with the same student, this time doing the opposite of each SOLAR tip. Have students identify the attributes that are missing. As a summary piece, make a copy of page 36 for each student. Have students illustrate each letter of SOLAR on their papers and write in the matching descriptors.

Spot-the-Sound Board Game

Students can practice listening for beginning, ending, and medial consonant and vowel sounds with this simple matching game.

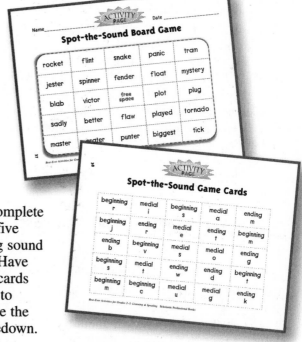

(◉) Photocopy the game board on page 37 and game cards on page 38 for each pair of players. The board features 24 words spread across rows and columns. The game cards list beginning, middle, and ending sounds. The first player to complete a row or column of five words with matching sound cards is the winner. Have students shuffle the cards and deal three cards to each player and place the remaining cards facedown.

(◉) Players take turns trying to match sound cards to words on the board. For example, a player with a "beginning *r*" sound card can place it on the board space labeled "rocket." Have students note that they might be able to place some cards on more than one space. They may also be able to put down more than one card (and they can).

(◉) After completing their turn, players pick up as many cards from the deck as they placed on the game board, so that they always have three cards.

(◉) The first player to complete a row or column of five words, horizontally, vertically, or diagonally, is the winner. It is important for players to realize that the winner is not necessarily the one who puts down the most cards but who completes the row or column. This can involve some strategic thinking as well as sound and letter recognition and matching. Remind students that it may not always be a good idea to place all of their cards down, even if they can.

Pack copies of the game board and game cards in resealable plastic bags for students to sign out and take home. Review directions with students who take home the game, or type up directions and include them in the bag.

Listening Aesthetically

Music provides the direction in a listening activity that invites an artistic response from students.

⎙ Give students sheets of large white drawing paper and various art materials such as markers, crayons, paints, and colored pencils.

⎙ Choose two musical recordings that are very much in contrast to each other.

⎙ Have students fold their papers in half. Explain to students that you will be playing some music for them and that you would like them to use the art materials to create a picture while they listen. The picture they create will be their illustration of the music.

⎙ Play the first musical selection several times so that students have enough time to hear and translate their impressions to the paper.

⎙ The following day, play the contrasting piece of music while the class uses the second half of their papers to respond to the new music. At the end of the session, ask students to open up their papers and compare and contrast the two illustrations. How are they different? How are they the same? How do their colors, shapes, styles, and subject matter reflect each musical selection?

Literature LINK

Georgia Music

by Helen V. Griffith (Greenwillow Books, 1986)

This fun and touching story tells of a young girl's visit with her grandfather in rural Georgia. He introduces her to the sounds of Georgia music: bumblebees bumbling, leaves touching each other, grasshoppers and crickets whirring and scratching, and so on. When her grandfather becomes ill and must leave Georgia to live in Baltimore with the girl and her mother, he is lonesome and lost until his granddaughter uses some Georgia music to bring him around. In a followup, ask students if there are sounds that make them feel comfortable, relaxed, or at home. Have them brainstorm a list. Contrast this with a list of sounds that make students feel uncomfortable, nervous, or scared. Discuss how various sounds can help set a mood or create a character in their writing.

Take-Home Activity:
Word Collectors

It's great to get parents and children involved in developing listening and word-building skills together. This simple activity is designed to get them doing just that.

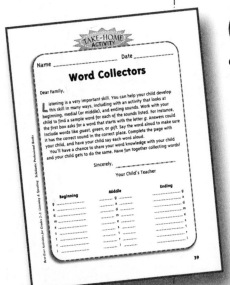

Give each student a copy of page 39. Review the chart, making sure that children know what kinds of words they're going to collect. You might try a couple in the classroom and model how to fill in the chart before students take the assignment home. When children return their papers to school, let them share the words they found. Record their findings on a master chart. How many different words did they find for the beginning *g* sound? middle *g* sound? ending *g* sound? Repeat for the other letters. You might post a class chart for each letter (one chart at a time) and let children continue finding and recording words that fit.

Literature
LINK

The Listening Walk

by Paul Showers (HarperCollins, 1991)

In this gently paced picture book, a girl takes a special kind of walk, during which she listens for the great variety of sounds around her. After hearing this story, you might want to take your students on a listening walk. Have them bring along pencils, paper, and a clipboard on which to write. Pause at various points along the way and let students write down some of the sounds they hear. After the walk, compare notes and list all of the sounds students heard.

White Elephant Auction

This activity emphasizes good speaking, writing, and listening in a fun context. It's great for the end of the year.

Explain that a white elephant is something that's silly, unwanted, and generally pretty useless. Invite students to bring in a white elephant object from home. Have them write a description of their object, describing how it could be used or how much fun it would be to have. This is a good activity for encouraging a sense of humor in students' writing voice. Once students have completed the writing, have a "Preview Day," as with a real auction. Arrange the objects, then let students take turns reading their descriptive writing piece to preview each piece. On Auction Day, model the bidding process and provide students with class currency to use. Students will need to listen carefully if they want to get that "special something."

Deborah Bauer
Mesa School District
Mesa, Arizona

Parts-of-Speech Word Stack

This simple but fun activity builds listening and speaking skills as students learn about parts of speech.

- Give each student three index cards. Ask students to write the following labels on the cards (one per card): "Noun," "Verb," and "Adjective."

- On a separate sheet of paper, have students list five words. Four of the words should be the same part of speech and one should be a different part of speech—for example, *cat, dog, boy, desk* (nouns), and *run* (verb).

- Let students take turns reading aloud their lists while the rest of the class listens (with their parts-of-speech cards in front of them) for the word that doesn't belong. When they hear the word, have them raise the card with the appropriate part of speech. In this way, everyone participates in every round, either as a presenter or listener. Let a student tell why the word didn't belong, then repeat the activity to let other students share their words.

Randi Mrvos
Home School Teacher
Lexington, Kentucky

As students learn new parts of speech, you can have them add cards to their stack.

It Fell in the Blender!

Learning phonetic concepts has a great deal to do with listening carefully for sounds. Blends are often a focus in second and third grade and are sometimes difficult for students to "hear." This "blender" activity provides some playful practice.

Make a copy of page 40 for each student. Randomly select and read target words from the teacher list (see left) and have students circle the blends on their papers. Wait. That's too easy. Well, the hard part is that these words have fallen in the blender and are all mixed up. Fortunately, the blend is intact but the rest of the letters are scrambled. Students must hear the word and find which mixed-up word fits the word you said aloud, then write it in the space.

Word List

blast
trade
flash
step

crate
fresh
brought
cleaning

greater
princess
blame
flamingo

stopping
trainer
crane
breakfast

clipper
frame
grass
printer

Sound Challenge

One of the challenges to listening carefully is background noise that interferes with what we are trying to hear. For example, you might be at an airport listening for a flight announcement but there are also people talking, luggage being wheeled by, and other distractions. Have students practice dealing with this by trying the Sound Challenge.

ⓢ Tell students that you are going to read aloud a math problem. This problem will be simple enough to solve mentally. They will not need to write anything down, but they must keep their eyes closed while listening. The first time you try this, do it without any interference. Let students share their answers.

ⓢ Now have some students be distractors. You might just ask them to have a loud conversation or supply them with musical or rhythm instruments to use.

ⓢ While your noisemakers provide the distractions, give the rest of the class another mental math problem to solve. Compare the results and share strategies for focusing even with background noise. You'll have to repeat the activity because everyone will want to take a turn making the distractor noise, providing more listening and math practice for everyone else!

Sequence Listening

Here's a way to practice targeted listening for a series of items.

Give students paper and pencils. Tell them you will be reading a list of items. The items may be numbers, words, or letters. You want them to write down the fourth one they hear. For example, if you say, "Chicago, Detroit, New York, Philadelphia, Los Angeles, Houston, Orlando," students would need to write down "Philadelphia," the fourth item in the list. You can make lists of all kinds of things, such as cities, states, and baseball teams. Alter the ordinal selected as well. After familiarizing students with the activity, let them make lists to read aloud. They really enjoy taking a turn leading the class and will gain some good practice with speaking skills, too!

What's in a Word?

Sometimes just one word can convey a lot of meaning. This connects with some of the more subtle ideas about listening. Not only do we listen to the word or words that are said but also to the way they are said. Have students experience this with a little playacting.

⊚ Ask for a volunteer. Have the student sit down in a chair at a desk. Give this child a play phone to use as a prop. Explain that the student will say one word into the phone, and in that word, will convey a specific meaning. Whisper a word to the volunteer (use the word *no* the first time), and tell that child the mood or feeling you want to convey, such as fear or happiness.

⊚ While the class listens, have the volunteer pick up the phone and say the word in such a way as to convey the intended mood. The volunteer can repeat the word as many times as he or she likes but can say only that word. Let students in the audience guess what the feeling is. How did they know? What kinds of things did they listen for?

⊚ Let students take turns at the phone. Simple words such as *yes, no, never,* and *sure* are effective, as are short phrases such as *of course, not now,* and *very soon.*

Wendy Wise-Borg
Rider University
Lawrenceville, New Jersey

Listening for Literary Elements

Learning about story elements fits very naturally into listening carefully to read-alouds.

There are many great picture book read-alouds for grades 2 and 3. Choose one to read to students, but before you do, introduce and discuss the elements of a story: character, setting (time and place), point of view, mood, and plot. The first time you read the story aloud, just read it as a story to enjoy. Then tell students you will be reading it aloud a second time, and this time you would like them to listen for the various story elements discussed. Ask them to take notes during the second reading. Follow up by discussing the various elements of the story. Encourage children to use their notes as they participate.

A favorite book for this activity is *Do Not Open,* by Brinton Turkle (Dutton, 1993).

Interview Introductions

This is a good activity for the beginning of the year. It helps students get to know each other and builds a cooperative atmosphere as they work together to create a short presentation.

⊚ Give each student a copy of page 41. Assign partners and have students move to quiet areas of the classroom or hall.

⊚ Have partners use the interview guide to gather information and notes about each other. As they ask questions, they should listen to the answers and take notes. (They'll be using their notes to introduce their partners to the class.)

⊚ When all students have finished this phase of the activity, have partners come up to the front of the room and take turns using their notes to introduce each other to the class. This allows students to be introduced to the class, without the added pressure of talking about themselves. It gives everyone great practice in speaking, listening, note-taking, and presenting. And by the end of the session, everyone knows a little bit more about their classmates.

Kinesthetic Clay Work

Combine creativity, listening, and some math with a project that taps into kinesthetic learning.

Give each student a chunk of clay. Tell the class you will be making sculptures together. Each sculpture will be different but will have some of the same elements, mainly certain three-dimensional shapes. Introduce the following shapes one at a time, having students follow your model and make them with their own clay: sphere, cylinder, cone, pyramid, cube, and rectangular prism. Have students describe what makes each shape distinctive, such as the number of sides, number of points, and shape of sides. After students have had a chance to practice making samples of each shape, describe the requirements of the sculpture: It must have two pyramids, one sphere, a rectangular prism, and two cylinders. These can be arranged in any manner students wish. (Record this information on the chalkboard.) After students have finished their sculptures, have them check their work to make sure it meets all the requirements. Then let them compare their artwork, noticing how even though everyone used the same shapes, the arrangements have resulted in very different final designs.

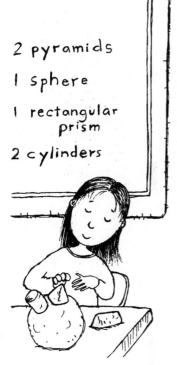

2 pyramids
1 sphere
1 rectangular prism
2 cylinders

Listening Interview

Listening is so intertwined with other skills, it's sometimes difficult to determine if there is a problem with listening or something else. For example, you may ask a student to circle the letter *g* on a paper and she may hear you fine but not be able to visually discriminate the written letter *g* from *d*. To isolate listening skills in an assessment, try an oral listening interview.

Meet one-on-one with a student and ask some simple questions that require only a verbal response. For example, try mentioning some simple words and ask the student to identify the initial, ending, and medial sounds. Is the student able to answer appropriately? How about when you lower your voice? How about if you turn your head and ask the question while looking away? If you suspect there is any sort of hearing problem, an early referral to the nurse for a quick check can be very helpful. Catching a hearing problem early on is key. If hearing is fine but listening is weak, you can provide extra activities in class and as homework to strengthen that skill.

The Music That Inspires Us

This is a good project to connect with a study you are doing about another country or culture.

Bring in a CD, record, or tape that features a particular type or style of music—for example, Brazilian, classical, country, or African. Play some selections for students and let them listen quietly. Then ask them to list things the music makes them think of. List these on the chalkboard. Next, tell students you are going to play the music again. This time ask students to think of any colors, images, or moods they "hear." Play the music again, then discuss and list the new ideas. Give students art paper and paints, markers, or crayons. Ask them to create a drawing or painting of some of the images that came to mind from the music. Display the artwork, and invite other classes to visit and view the art while the "music that inspired us" plays in the background.

Sound and Setting

Setting is an important part of any story. Have students do a little experimental writing with setting through sound.

Play a recording of a sound such as rain, or make a sound for students, such as the beating of a drum or the impatient tapping of a pencil. Explain to students that you would like them to begin their story with this sound. This will help provide the setting or mood. Although all stories will begin with the same sound and opening, they almost always all develop and turn out differently. It is also interesting for students to note that sound is an effective way to draw the reader into the story with an immediacy that touches the reader's senses.

In the News

Reporters are supposed to give us the five W's (who, what, when, where, why) and an H (how). Do they always? Use a real-life activity to build listening skills and bone up on current events.

- Cut out some newspaper articles. Explain to students that you will be reading aloud an article. You want them to listen for answers to these questions: who, what, when, where, why, and how.

- Give each child a copy of page 42. Have students listen carefully to your reading of the article and write down quick notes that answer very simply and basically the six questions.

- Follow up by having students share what they heard and recorded.

- Now read the news article again so that students can check their accuracy against the story one more time.

- Repeat the activity a few times a week, having students keep their record sheets together. Encourage them to compare their answers to the questions over time. Are they becoming better listeners? How can they tell?

SECOND Language LEARNERS

Much of the information we get on a daily basis about the news, weather, sports, or events comes to us from listening to the radio or television. Many of the phrases, expressions, and idioms can be very confusing to second-language learners. A classic example is "raining cats and dogs." For a homework assignment, ask families of all students to listen to a radio or TV news program together. (Remind families to be aware of the content and to choose something that is appropriate for their children.) Ask them to write down any phrases or words that are idiomatic expressions—that can't be understood by looking at the meaning of the word(s) alone—and to bring them to class. Discuss the idioms or expressions; there are many examples that even native English speakers will have little understanding of. Make copies of page 43. Let students compile the expressions in an illustrated class reference book that all can use.

KidsTime Deluxe (Great Wave Software) includes activities that are especially good for working on listening skills. For example, "Story Writer" converts selected text to pictures or pictures to text. When a story has been completed, the computer will "read" it back to the writer so the writer can listen.

Interactive Morning Message:
Sound of the Day

Start the day with a morning message that invites careful listening and a little fun.

Before class starts, record a common sound on an audiotape—for example, a doorbell or car horn. Write a morning message that invites students to listen to the sound and record a guess about what it is. After everyone has arrived and had a chance to respond, bring students together around the tape player. Play the sound again and identify it. Repeat the activity other mornings, using more difficult sounds, such as the hum of a refrigerator or the sound of a pencil moving across a paper. Invite students to create their own sound tapes to be featured as "Sound of the Day."

Take-Home Activity:
Listen Together

This take-home activity pack is designed to foster a school-home connection, while promoting read-alouds, listening, and reading responses.

Label a large resealable plastic bag "Take-Home Activity Pack: Listen Together." Place two age-appropriate picture books as well as a laminated copy of page 44 (a letter to families) and a copy of page 45 (reading response sheet) in the bag. Include a special pencil. (Stickers might be fun, too.) Let children take turns signing it out to share at home. Allow families at least a few days to fit in the activities before asking for the activity pack to be returned. Consider making several copies of the activity pack so that there's less wait time for children to take it home.

Sounds of Poetry

With this activity students learn that there's more than one way to listen to a poem.

- Give children copies of the poem "Sounds" on page 46. Read the poem aloud, asking students to listen for words that describe how things sound. When you're finished reading the poem, invite children to recall some of those words—for example, *tinkling, buzzing,* and *crunching.*

- Divide the class into small groups. Try to have one group for each sound represented in the poem. Let each group choose a sound from the poem to explore. For example, what would "happy play" sound like? How about "the sound September brings"?

- Give children time to create and practice their sounds. Then bring the class together for another reading. This time, have children make the sound effects at the appropriate times. Compare the two readings. How did students listen the first time? (*by imagining the sounds*) How did they listen the second time? (*by hearing the sounds*)

Easy Listening

Sometimes listening can be difficult. Why? There are lots of things that can interfere. The listener might be tired, the subject might be boring, or the speaker might be going too fast. Use this activity to help students learn what to do when they're having a tough time listening.

Ask students to make two lists: one for things that make listening difficult and one for things that promote good listening. Let students share their lists. Use their ideas to guide a discussion about how students can improve both their speaking and listening abilities. For example, if students understand that talking too fast makes listening difficult, they can set a goal for themselves to slow down when they speak. You might want to generate two charts that summarize students' ideas and use them as references for speakers and listeners.

Clap and Repeat

Sound often appears in patterns—for example, the "Beep! Beep! Beep!" of a clock alarm and the barking of a dog. Use the idea of sound patterns in a listening game.

Have students listen carefully to clapping patterns that you present. Begin with simple patterns, such as "clap, clap (pause), clap." Have students repeat the pattern they hear. Make patterns more complex as listening and repeating become more skilled. Add in variations such as finger snapping, knee slapping, or desk tapping. Have students come up with their own variations and lead the class in new patterns. This is a great way to get students' attention. Whenever you begin a pattern of clapping, everyone stops and repeats the pattern. This has students looking, listening, and emptying their hands at the same time so that their focus is complete.

Everyone's Responsibility

It is not uncommon to have a few students who participate in class but in such a way that it is difficult to hear them. Most often, the rest of the class ignores what the hard-to-hear student has said and the teacher ends up asking the student to speak more loudly, slowly, or clearly. Try a different approach to help involve the rest of the class through shared responsibility.

Make it clear that whatever is said in discussion, everyone will be responsible for. For example, if John says the answer is "George Washington," everyone in the class is responsible for hearing John's answer and being able to repeat it. If John speaks too softly, the other students are responsible for asking John in a way that exhibits good manners what it is he said or to please repeat it so all can hear. Model and practice this a few times before making it a standing requirement. You will find that having students work together on this encourages peers to improve their presentation and discussion skills as well as their listening skills.

Evan Milman
Maurice Hawk School
Princeton Junction, New Jersey

Silly Syllables, Extraordinary Words

Syllabication helps students with reading, listening, and pronunciation. Choose some target words with a variety of syllables and use them to strengthen these skills.

Say a word aloud and ask students to listen for the number of syllables. Have them say the word back and clap out the syllables. For example, *piano* would get three claps, one on each syllable (pi-an-o). Practice this with a number of words, then let students come up with words that have one, two, three, and four syllables and lead the class in clapping them out. After students become proficient with this, let them have some fun by creating words of their own. You might want to use some of Dr. Seuss's as examples; he has coined plenty. Have students create the word, break it up into syllables, write a definition, and illustrate it. Compile students' pages into a class dictionary of Extraordinary Words.

Literature LINK

Ruby Mae Has Something to Say

by David Small (Crown, 1992)

Miss Ruby Mae Foote is tongue-tied until her young nephew, Billy Bob, invents a special hat, the Bobatorn, that gives her enough confidence in public speaking that she leaves the little town of Nada, Texas, and goes to speak before the United Nations. She delivers a "straight talk" message to the world, but only after a last-minute rescue by her enterprising nephew. After reading the story, invite students to compose a very short "straight talk" speech they would like to share with the world. Limit students to four sentences. (Ruby Mae used only two.) Have students take turns presenting their short speeches to the class. Help summarize the book and activity by asking "Can you share an important idea in a short speech? Did Ruby Mae? Did the class?"

Robot Instruction Writing

As teachers, we are always giving instructions. Students love having a turn at this and it can be a good opportunity for practice in clear thinking, reading, writing, and listening.

Have students partner up. One partner will be the instructor, the other the robot. The instructor chooses a simple task for the robot to do. It might be tying a shoe or adding two numbers together on paper. The instructor must write out instructions on how to do this task. The instructions must be very clear and specific because the robot can only do exactly what the instructor says—no more, no less. The robot then listens carefully to the instructions and follows along. The instructor may need to adjust instructions after seeing the results of the first trial. After several trials, have partners switch roles. This is fun for all, and it really helps students see that words need to be specific and clear for the listener.

TIP

You can place certain parameters on participation, such as "Use only two sentences" or "Remain in the same setting."

Story Circle

Students pass a story along in an activity that builds creative storytelling skills and encourages attentive listening.

Gather students in a seated circle. Begin telling a story. You might say something like "Joanne had never been to the cave before. She had always been curious about it but had never had a chance to visit till today." Now "pass" the story (you can use a book or piece of paper to physically represent the story) to the student next to you. This student continues the story, then passes it to the next child, and so on around the circle. Students have to listen carefully as the story moves so they can add a piece that is consistent with what has come before. This is a really fun way to focus listening, and stories can turn out to be very interesting and creative. (Consider tape-recording them. Students will love revisiting their stories!)

Mrs. Brown, She Had a Class...

Students learn most songs they sing simply by listening. "Old MacDonald" is one they'll remember.

Write the words to "Old MacDonald" on a chart. (See right.) Now have fun with the song. Replace some of the words to make it a little more individualized. So, if your name is Mrs. Brown, the song might go like this:

Mrs. Brown, she had a class
A-B-C-D-E.
And in her class
There was (insert student name)
A-B-C-D-E.
With a (insert something the student likes to do or is known for) here
And a _____, _____ there.
Here a _____, there a _____,
Everywhere a _____, _____.
Mrs. Brown, she had a class,
A-B-C-D-E.

Have students write their own verses to share something about themselves. Students will really listen and sing along as this innovative song comes together.

Old MacDonald
had a farm
E-I-E-I-O.
And on his farm
He had a pig
E-I-E-I-O.
With an oink,
oink here
And an oink,
oink there.
Here an oink,
There an oink,
Everywhere an
oink, oink.
Old MacDonald
had a farm
E-I-E-I-O.

Literature LINK

Too Much Noise

by Ann McGovern (Houghton Mifflin, 1967)

A farmer suffers in a house that he believes is too noisy. There are noises from little things like the wind coming through the cracks and the tea kettle whistling. The farmer goes to a wise man for help. The wise man counsels him to bring various animals to live in the house with him. Things obviously get even noisier. Children will have fun joining in on all the various sounds that are repeated throughout the story.

Sound Board

Here's a challenging but fun listening activity students will enjoy again and again.

Give each child a copy of the Sound Board, an assortment of 20 different blends and digraphs. (See page 47.) You may want to laminate these to make them reusable, or run additional copies as needed. Tell students you will be saying some words and you would like them to find the box on their Sound Board that has a corresponding sound (specify blend or digraph). Then write the number in that box that corresponds to the order in which the word was said. For example, if the first word you say is *cross*, students will write a 1 in the box with the *cr* blend. Keep a list of the words you say and mark your own copy of the Sound Board as you go. Check the numbers together when you're finished. You can choose the phonetic features you want to focus on and use the corresponding number of words. (Students won't necessarily fill up the board each time you play.)

TIP

Let students arrange their Alliteration Land papers on a bulletin board. Or for a more creative display, let students cut out each building and arrange it, along with roads and other features, to create one giant Alliteration Land.

Alliteration Land

Students enjoy playing with alliterative language. This activity lets them create a town based on the concept of alliteration.

⊚ Share some examples of alliteration from stories. Guide students to recognize that alliteration is a series of words that have the same beginning sound. You might also mention stores, companies, and products that use alliteration to catch people's attention. After all, who wouldn't be interested in Cousin Keith's Crunchy Cookies?

⊚ Tell students they are going to have a chance to try out some alliterative writing on their own. As you give out copies of Alliteration Land (see page 48), explain that students should fill in the sign on each building with an alliterative name. (They can decide what their buildings are—schools, shops, stores, libraries, restaurants, and so on.) Have students draw the product or service offered in the windows.

Stepping Into Stories

Let students step into their favorite stories with Readers Theater productions—a natural for enriching literature studies and promoting speaking and listening skills.

Readers Theater is a great way to help children develop their abilities to read with expression, practice presentation skills, and provide an audience with wonderful listening opportunities. You can purchase prepared Readers Theater scripts, but it is just as easy to adapt appropriate books. The Arthur series, by Marc Brown (Little, Brown), works particularly well. These books feature lots of dialogue and plenty of characters. Provide multiple copies of one of these titles and let children work in groups to prepare presentations.

One or two students in each group can be narrators. These narrators will read any writing that is not in quotation marks. Other students in each group can play the various characters. Have students practice reading the story aloud in their small groups several times before presenting to the class. Remind students that with Readers Theater, there is no need for motions, props, or scenery, just good, clear reading and lots of expression. The audience will be listening to their voices only. In fact, a good culminating activity is to tape-record Readers Theater presentations so they can be heard again and again or used in conjunction with the book for interested readers.

Looking for ready-to-use scripts? Author Aaron Shepard's Web site (**www.aaron shep.com**) features dozens of Readers Theater scripts. You'll also find detailed how-tos for scripting, staging, and performing Readers Theater productions.

SECOND Language LEARNERS

As students learn a new language, many times they will be able to obtain meaning early on by focusing on key words. Practice this idea by acting out small scenes. An example might be a restaurant. Your students want to know the price of a hot dog. What key words will they be listening for in a response? Money words. Number words. If the waiter responds, "Hot dogs are on special today: only 99 cents." Students do not need to understand "special," but if they hear "99 cents," they will have the answer to their question. Have students suggest scenarios in which they might need help. Generate lists of possible key vocabulary that would be important for places such as restaurants, malls, cafeterias, movies, sporting events, libraries, and so on. Review these words and use them as you act out the scenes. When students encounter the real thing, they will be much better prepared.

Name _____ Date _____

SOLAR Graphic Organizer

Write a sentence that describes what each letter stands for.

S _____

O _____

L _____

A _____

R _____

Name _____

Date _____

Spot-the-Sound Board Game

rocket	flint	snake	panic	tram
jester	spinner	fender	float	mystery
blab	victor	**free space**	plot	plug
sadly	better	flaw	played	tornado
master	crater	punter	biggest	tick

ACTIVITY PAGE

Spot-the-Sound Game Cards

beginning r	medial i	beginning s	medial a	ending m
beginning j	ending r	medial e	ending t	beginning m
ending b	beginning v	medial s	medial o	ending g
beginning s	medial t	ending w	ending d	beginning t
beginning m	beginning c	medial u	medial g	ending k

Best-Ever Activities for Grades 2–3: Listening & Speaking Scholastic Professional Books

Name _____ Date _____

Word Collectors

Dear Family,

Listening is a very important skill. You can help your child develop this skill in many ways, including with this activity. Work with your child to find a sample word for each of the sounds listed. For instance, the first box asks for a word that starts with the letter *g*. Answers could include words like *guest*, *green*, or *gift*. Say the word aloud to make sure it has the correct sound in the correct place. Complete the page with your child, and have your child say each word aloud.

   You'll have a chance to share your word knowledge with your child and your child gets to do the same. Have fun together collecting words!

Sincerely,

_____

Your Child's Teacher

Beginning	Middle	Ending
g	g	g
a	a	a
d	d	d
m	m	m
e	e	e
s	s	s
t	t	t
r	r	r
i	i	i

It Fell in the Blender!

stabl	edtra	sflah	pest
acret	shefr	obrguth	nneaclgi
aetergr	sprencis	blema	ogflmani
gponipst	retrina	crena	akstebrfa
preclpi	amfre	sgras	iretprn

Interviewer's Name _____ Date _____

Interview Guide

I am interviewing _____ .

Age _____

Hobbies, Sports, and Activities _____

_____

Favorite Foods _____

_____

Favorite Books _____

_____

Favorite Movies _____

_____

Dislikes _____

_____

Something Else to Share _____

_____

Name _____ Date _____

In the News

Who, what, when, where, why, and *how*? These are some of the things you can learn in a news story. Listen to the news story your teacher reads. Jot down information that answers each question.

Title of the Article _____

Reporter _____

Who? _____

What? _____

When? _____

Where? _____

Why? _____

How? _____

TRY THIS!

On your own paper, write a news story about something that happened at school or at home. Does your story answer *who, what, when, where, why,* and *how*?

Name _____   Date _____

Radio and TV Listening

Word or Phrase _____

What does it mean? _____

_____

_____

_____

Illustration

Use it in a sentence. _____

_____

Name _____   Date _____

Listen Together

Dear Family,

It is your turn to have the Listen Together Take-Home Activity Pack. Enclosed you will find two books, a pencil, and a response sheet. You and your child will use the materials to read, write, and listen together. You go first. Choose one of the books to read aloud to your child. Give your child one of the reading response sheets and have him or her write a response to the story. Invite your child to share the response with you. Then discuss the book together. The next night, it is your turn to be the listener. Have your child read the second book to you. This time, you write a response and discuss it with your child. Compare the two books and share favorite parts, characters, illustrations, and so on.

   Using these materials will give your child a valuable experience sharing ideas about books with you. It will also enable your child to see the value of reading, writing, and listening. Please return all materials in the bag after completing the activities. Enjoy, and thanks for participating!

                    Sincerely,

                    _____

                    Your Child's Teacher

Best-Ever Activities for Grades 2–3: Listening & Speaking   Scholastic Professional Books

Name _____   Date _____

Listen Together

Book 1	Book 2
1. Family Reading Partner	**1.** Family Reading Partner
_____	_____
2. Book	**2.** Book
_____	_____
3. Author	**3.** Author
_____	_____
4. Illustrator	**4.** Illustrator
_____	_____
5. Response to the Story	**5.** Response to the Story
_____	_____
_____	_____
_____	_____
_____	_____

Name _____ Date _____

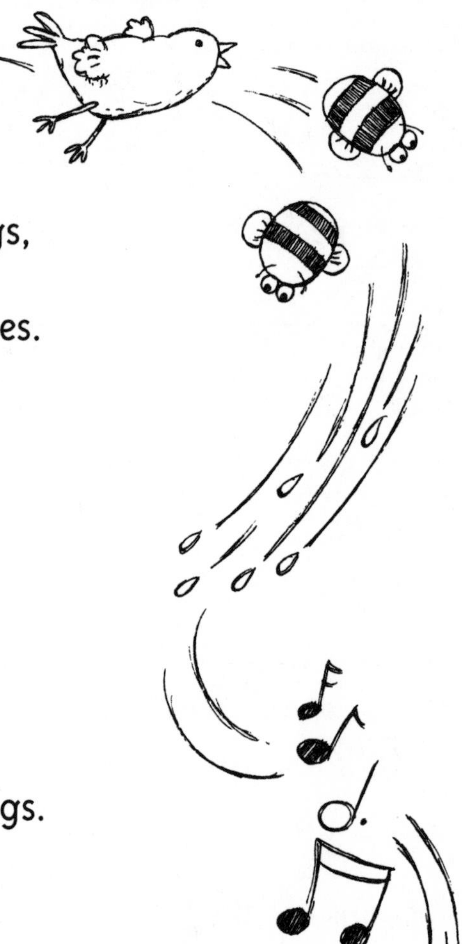

Sounds

I like the sound of many things—
Of tinkling streams, a bird that sings,
Of falling raindrops, buzzing bees,
Of crunching snow, and wind in trees.

I like the sound of happy play,
Of echoes soft and far away,
Of music gay or sweet and slow,
Of trains and cars that swiftly go.

But there is one sound nicer far
To me than all those others are;
I like the sound September brings
When once again the school bell rings.

—M. Lucille Ford

"SOUNDS" by M. Lucille Ford from Poetry Place
Anthology (Scholastic, 1990).

Best-Ever Activities for Grades 2–3: Listening & Speaking   Scholastic Professional Books

46

Name _____   Date _____

Sound Board

☐ cr	☐ br	☐ cl	☐ bl
☐ gr	☐ gl	☐ dr	☐ fr
☐ fl	☐ pr	☐ pl	☐ st
☐ tr	☐ sm	☐ sp	☐ wh
☐ sh	☐ ch	☐ th	☐ dr

Name _____

Date _____

Alliteration Land

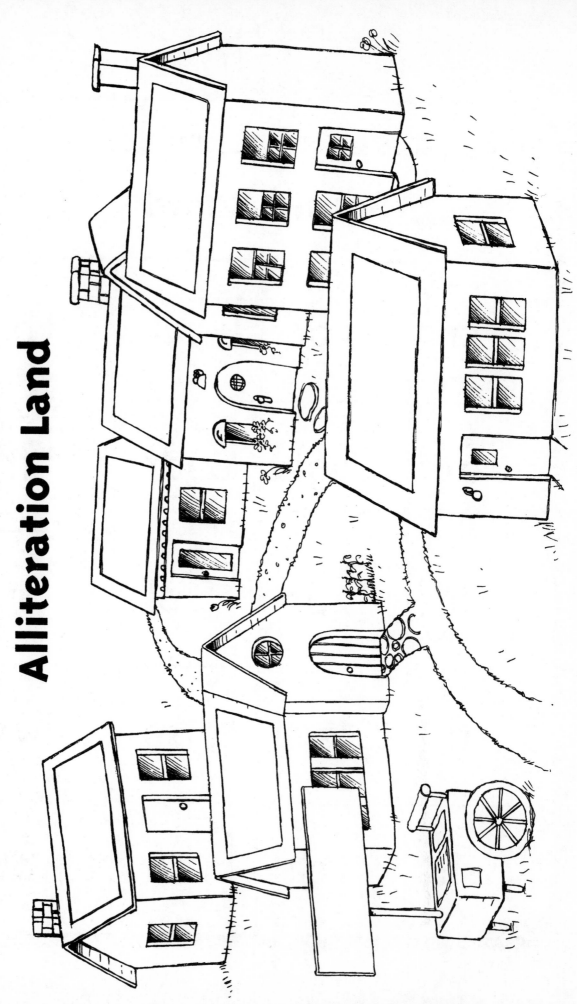

Best-Ever Activities for Grades 2–3: Listening & Speaking   Scholastic Professional Books